I'd like to thank God for having allowed me to finish this book.

How to Do Marketing

Juan Manuel Rodríguez Caamaño

jmrc@us.edu.mx

About the author:

- Born in Mexico, in the city of Coatzacoalcos, Veracruz, on June 4, 1976.
- Holds a Bachelor's Degree in Marketing by the Instituto Tecnológico y de Estudios Superiores de Monterrey (ITESM), Monterrey Campus.
- Holds a Master's Degree in Business Administration by the Universidad Nacional Autónoma de México (UNAM).
- He is a Doctor of Education Sciences by the University of Havana (UH) in Cuba.
- Is a research professor at Universidad de Sotavento.
- Is the founding rector of Universidad Istmo Americana.
- Has published six scholarly books in the fields of marketing and administration, three of them as co-author:

  - *Auditoría Administrativa.* México: Editorial Gasca, 2008.
  - *Lobbying y Cabildeo: un enfoque social para el marketing y comunicación organizacional.* Editorial Gasca, 2008.
  - *Educación Física: Métodos para el trabajo con el adulto mayor.* Editorial Gasca, 2013.
  - *Cómo revertir la deserción universitaria.* Amazon, 2015.
  - *Cómo revertir la deserción universitaria II.* Amazon, 2015.
  - *Cómo hacer marketing.* Amazon, 2015

- He also has two novels published:

  - *Psicoaffaire: del amor y la muerte, su paso breve.* Amazon. 2015.
  - *Ciclos.* Amazon. 2015.

3 Reasons for Reading this Book

1) Profitability. The main reason to read this book is that the marketing concepts covered in it have been put into practice by the author in the business world, with great economic results, as evidenced by the growth of the different organizations in which he participates.

2) Consistency. All of these concepts have been used not once, but many times, always yielding positive results, thus proving that the marketing theory referenced in this book is functional for every field, and it is not just a matter of luck or chance. This document describes different scenarios in which the author's decision-making process is successful.

3) Simplicity. This material is quite simple to read, in that over less than 40 pages it makes an analysis of relevant information from the marketing gurus, which the author uses for his day-to-day management tasks. This is not your ordinary, complex, 600-page, boring marketing book.

Contents

Introduction

Most marketing experts are scholars who have long done research and who have spent many years sharing a great deal of knowledge that is poured in this book. The difference with this material is that I guarantee that if you use all of the information in these pages, you will find success in every area you apply it to.

Why you ask? Because I know from personal experience that every time I've applied this knowledge, it has worked, always to great results.

What results?

1. I graduated, thank goodness, on June 4, 1999. On that day, I turned 23. I didn't have a job, I didn't have a girlfriend, and I hadn't achieved anything relevant in my short life. Something rather incomprehensible for someone who is knowledgeable in marketing and who knows a thing or two about the art of selling. At that moment, I decided to start working in the family business, a private higher-education institution named Universidad de Sotavento. Everything was going just fine when I became the head of the marketing department, then I started thinking that I had to apply what I had learned in school to put my parents' investment in my university education to work. I was aware that what was being done at that point still had room for improvement, even if it was already yielding good results. By 2001, enrollment increased exponentially, thanks to a marketing program that was developed based on our first market research of the sector. I have always been an advocate for basing every marketing decision on information, and this time, it wasn't an exception. After applying the most complex research techniques and the most diverse statistical analysis methods to find the link between the variables of educational marketing, we obtained the most valuable information to solve the issue of increasing demand through a quite simple exploratory research. Once we had collected and correlated all kinds of information from our students—which still did not answer our question of how to boost enrollment—we launched a brief exploratory

research consisting of two simple questions asked to a sample of the city's population.

— Do you know about Universidad de Sotavento?

9 out of 10 answered 'Yes.'

— Have you ever been at Universidad de Sotavento?

9 out of 10 answered 'No.'

After much research and analysis done with the most complex tools, the issue was solved with those two simple questions.

It was clear that the school's publicity was working wonders since most people were aware of the brand, but very few knew about the high-quality product that we were offering. Years of investing resources in facilities, multiple laboratories, an extensive library, a large cafeteria, sports facilities, and green areas, and only a small number of the population knew about the product we had.

It was then that we developed a marketing plan in which the university would host all kinds of academic, social, cultural, athletic, and even religious events. This basic strategy resulted in a record-breaking enrollment of more than one thousand students in one school year, thanks to which the University was one of the highest growing universities in the country. This was according to the figures of the Mexican Ministry of Education (Secretaría de Educación Pública), which were published in the nation-wide distribution magazine, *Expansión*, where Universidad de Sotavento was ranked as one of the fastest-growing higher education institutions.

2. We marketers always want to increase the number of customers. Back in 2001, the market of students demanding a bachelor's degree from Universidad de Sotavento seemed saturated, and the number of applicants to higher education was rising steadily, but now there were more universities in the competition.

Once again, we resolved to use marketing and its concepts to increase the market. We couldn't lower the price of the line of products of the Sotavento brand since doing so could mean damage to its position as a leading academic institution. What we did was develop a new brand with different characteristics—a strictly academic establishment, with a unique academic offering, programs with a common duration, and a greater choice of degree conferral possibilities. As a result, Universidad Istmo Americana was created, and in 2008 it had an enrollment of 800 students for the school year, this was in response to the correct marketing decisions made during the previous years.

3. With two solid higher education institutions running—Universidad de Sotavento and the Universidad Istmo Americana—we questioned ourselves: how could we increase the number of clients, when the demand from higher education students was not increasing? Should we try relationship marketing? Should we develop new products for our existing customers?

That is how in 2002 the Postgraduate Department was created, to lengthen the stay of the students in the institution by continuing their studies with a Master's Degree—extending the life cycle of the product by creating master's programs, specialization courses, diploma courses, seminars, doctorate programs. At the same time, we were contributing to the quality of the main service that was offered, by training the university's professors. It was, undoubtedly, a full-fledged 'win-win' situation.

4. Another decision made to increase the customer base was opening campuses in other cities, this resulted in the opening of three Universidad de Sotavento campuses, and another three of Universidad Istmo Americana.

5. In 2012, the market was further expanded with new users by starting offering other education levels in the different campuses: kindergarten, middle school, open-ended and online high school.

6. The academic product was further enhanced in 2013 by opening within the universities' premises the English learning franchise, Harmon Hall.

Each of these achievements—plus many others that I cannot call my own, but the making of God and marketing—allow me to guarantee that every concept and experience shared in this book do actually work to accomplish business success.

And if the reader still wonders what happened with my situation of not having a girlfriend, I can say that the marketing concepts described in this document also worked in persuading and convincing another kind of market.

With this book you are purchasing a handbook for business success, I hope you enjoy it.

How to do marketing?

It is the first day of the Theory of Marketing class in the last semester of the Marketing program at Universidad de Sotavento. It is the perfect environment for the future leaders in this vast field of knowledge.

What is marketing?

The obvious question I make as I show a slide with the definitions of marketing given by the leading exponents.

Here are a few of the key concepts:

First by Philip Kotler, the most distinguished author in marketing: "Marketing is the social process by which individuals and groups obtain what they need and want through creating and exchanging products and value with others."

The American Marketing Association defines it: "Marketing is the process of planning and executing the conception, pricing, promotion, and distribution of ideas, goods, and services to create exchanges that satisfy individual and organizational objectives."

While William Stanton says: "Marketing is a total system of business activities designed to plan, price, promote, and distribute goods and services which can satisfy the wants of current and potential customers."

Even though these definitions may use different wording to express exactly the same, they all share a common implicit or explicit component: exchange.

The author of this book thinks the ideal definition of marketing is: "Marketing is building confidence."

As simple as that, marketing is about building confidence and, further ahead, once we include the marketing elements described throughout this chapter, we will demonstrate this definition.

What is the purpose of marketing?

My favorite definition of what marketing, as a science, should do; the most descriptive and perhaps the most romantic is:

"The purpose of marketing is to make selling superfluous. The aim of marketing is to know and understand customers so well that the product or service fits them and sells itself. In theory, the result of marketing should be customers ready to buy. All it takes, then, is to make the product or service available to them."

-Peter Drucker

In few words, if the endeavor of understanding your customer so well becomes essential for making marketing decisions, anything that is exchanged will be a perfect fit for your market segment. This will push the obsession of selling to the backburner because sales will happen automatically by understanding the market.

To understand the customer, we need to describe and tell the difference between these three concepts: needs, wants, and demand, which Kotler defined as follows:

- **Needs. Are the basic requirements that people have.**

- **Wants. Are aimed at specific objects that may satisfy a need.**

- **Demand. Are wants for specific products that are backed by an ability to pay for them.**

To Kotler, needs have existed since before marketers came to be. These needs become wants when they are aimed at specific items that may satisfy the need. Marketers, together with other influences of society, have an effect on wants. Therefore, a good understanding of the customer is trying to predict their purchasing behavior and the surrounding variables to influence their decision so that they channel their needs to the products that marketing wants them to buy. Which is why it is critical to know what their needs are.

When we speak of needs, the most widely referenced authors are Maslow, McClelland, and Herzberg. Although speaking in marketing terms, Maslow makes a better attempt at describing the characteristics inherent to satisfaction, and even allows to understand how one single product can satisfy different needs for each individual or group of individuals that make up a market segment.

This is Maslow's hierarchy of needs, his most relevant theory:

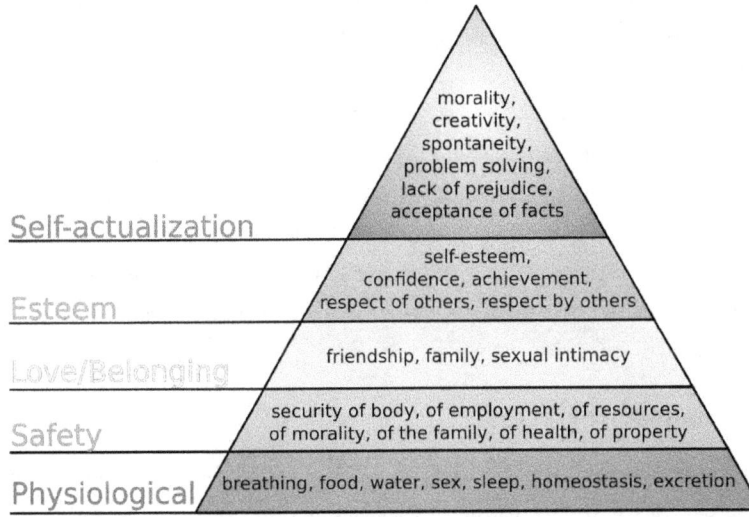

The importance lies in knowing how we can make an influence to make our product satisfy every need.

For example, a mobile phone satisfies the need for family safety, since one can get hold of their children. It also gives us employment security by having digitalized documents at hand. It gives us a sense of belonging by knowing we can have many groups of friends to communicate with via SMS, Pin, social networks or Whatsapp. It can even take us to self-actualization, by having an exclusive piece of equipment that not many people have access to.

A single product may satisfy different needs, which is why it is important to determine which need is being satisfied by each product. We could segment a market following a specific characteristic, to develop a more effective and specific marketing strategy that works from the consumers' needs and not from their purchasing behavior or their characteristics as a market.

A student in class questions me about mobile phone use, saying they have become a necessity, no longer a want, since they were supposedly only satisfying the need for communication and today it has become essential for most people to own a mobile phone when in the past they didn't have that need. I smile back, answering that those who should be worried about this are the products that are being replaced by mobile phones because smartphones are satisfying a wide array of needs. There are people who can't leave home without their mobile phone because it is their mobile office while others can't because it is how they communicate with friends. It is not that marketing creates a need by having people walk by a store window displaying mobile phones; but rather a smart marketer understands the customers so well that, before any other product or brand, he's made available to them an option to satisfy their need for self-esteem, acknowledgment, love, belonging, safety, etc.

The marketing process

An obvious question for every marketer, which might not have come to mind during their school years, is: if you had to define marketing as a process, how would you do it?

And it is a matter of common sense or logic—as everything in marketing is—because they always come up with the right answer. Most of the future holders of a degree in marketing talk of a process as the one shown in Figure 1. The first step, for every marketing lover, is information: the key to understanding our customer in its true dimension.

Figure 1. The marketing process

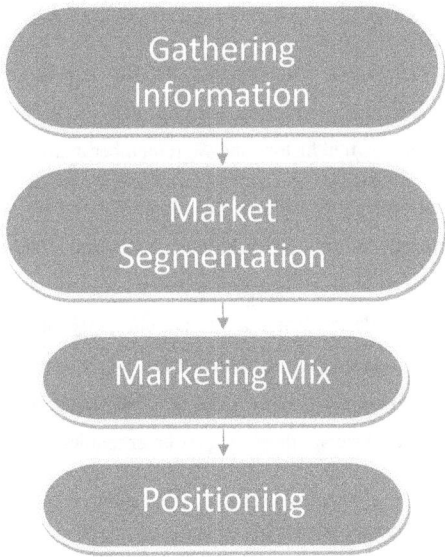

This leads to the first of my basic principles of marketing: if you are making decisions without information, you are not doing marketing.

How can we fully understand our customer?

The previous mobile phone example, where Information and Communication Technologies (ICT) start replacing many needs virtually, gives us an idea of the importance of fully understanding customers or cease existing as a brand.

One Christmas, I realized it didn't matter how much money I spent trying to please my son, Johnny. At that time, I gifted him with a toy car, which was nearly a replica of a real car. It was equipped with a battery, and it accelerated and braked as a life-sized car does. I paid a fortune for the toy, but it was only amusing for a couple of days. Every Christmas, all the expensive gifts had the same fate. Every day would be a day-long tantrum from the boy because he wanted to play with his mom's tablet, and he would quarrel to buy inexpensive games, which surely have a greater reach because they are distributed digitally and get to wherever around the world where there is internet access.

By noting this, I realized toy manufacturers have two ways to go: either they get better at understanding their customers—children—or they will end up being one more toy in the pile of products that go down in history and we remember many years later with nostalgia.

You, my reader, have every right of questioning me about what should be done to understand the customers so well and be able to reverse the effect of children preferring to play with a tablet than with actual toys. I have an easy way out: I am lucky not to be part of the toy industry because the challenge ahead is quite hefty and this industry has to focus every action into understanding the customer better than the substitute product, or they are going to have to find something else to do. One quite successful marketer has already molded children's wants to satisfy their need for entertainment with a tablet.

What is needed now is more talented decision-makers who are able to make this want evolve into wants for products specific to their brands. This is a huge task considering children's game developers have already such a great understanding of their customers that kids can now design the players, name them whatever they wish, build the playing environment, attach their own image—all this in order to customize the game, play by themselves or against other players from around the world, play the game remotely, and become a part of the game by moving synchronized to other players.

Wow! This is such a complicated scenario for the entertainment business, although it seems someone has really grasped the infinite creativity of children.

Step 1. Gathering information

Whether you want to enter the market of an existing product, or of a new one, the first step is gathering information to make marketing decisions. Speaking in broad terms, and summing up the most widely regarded research methodology theories, there are four ways of gathering information from the market.

The four data sources may be used all at once, or as needed, to collect enough information and make the right decisions:

- **Primary data sources:** Primary data is collected specifically for the purpose of the project at hand, and may be obtained by:

    1. Survey: consisting of making questions directly to the target population of the research;

    2. Observation: consisting of observing and recording the behavior of the target population of the research; and

    3. Experimentation: consisting of reproducing certain stimuli within a variable-controlled laboratory, to a specific group of people, to then see the difference compared to a group not exposed to the stimuli.

    4. The fourth tool for gathering information are:

- **Secondary data sources:** that is information already available that has been gathered for another purpose (Stanton).

An example of secondary data collection would be carrying out a documentary analysis, namely, going over documents already published about my product; or conducting a bibliographic review of information already existing—books, thesis, scientific articles—that are related to my product or to my research.

In a nutshell, if we wish to collect data to have information that gives us more precision during the decision-making process, we could ask (survey), observe (observation), experiment (experimentation), and/or go over the information already gathered (documentary analysis).

Step 2. Market Segmentation

Segmentation is the second step in marketing which has been analyzed by many authors, with different approaches and names. Take Al Ries and his theory, which is closely related to the concept of dividing into segments, of being different. In brief, it is necessary to identify precisely who our target market is, and how we want to approach it in a structured way—including what we have learned about the segmentation variables that exist—because all of this is the foundation for an effective marketing strategy, with effective designs, that can achieve its purpose.

What do we segment for?

- To have a strategy that is a perfect fit for the needs of the market.

- To assess what segments of the whole market are the most profitable and viable for the company by analyzing, among other factors, its size and saturation. Maybe a market is large, but with a low purchasing power; or is a very large market with a high purchasing power but with a high saturation, that is, many competitors, which decreases the size of demand. Perhaps the market is still profitable, but too large or limited for our brand to satisfy its demand.

- To visualize segments that are not desirable.

- To save time by focusing the strategy.

- To become specialized in the attention of the target market and be able to develop relationship marketing and build consumer loyalty.

- To determine what markets could be profitable by making variations of the strategy with a minimum investment. In a nutshell, to maximize profits. It may turn out, for example that the exact same product, with a different brand and a different distribution channel, allows us to discover a whole new market sector, or at a different price, or with a different promotion strategy to satisfy more markets that are still profitable for the company.

- To know who our direct competitors are, which could be all the substitute products that exist within that market.

- To save in production, promotion and distribution expenses, by properly guiding the strategy.

Types of segmentation in consumer markets

Focusing on certain characteristics of the market, it may be segmented as follows:

- Geographically: For example, by city, neighborhood, area, postal code, block, street.

- Demographically: Some authors call it socio-demographic segmentation. For example, by income, age, gender, marital status, the level of education, social class, etc.

- Psychographically: Grouping characteristics that are related to the Values and Life Styles of people, their attitudes, feelings, and creeds. The VALS 1 and 2 tests were designed to group the North American population into the following segments:

  1. By self-orientation

  - Principle oriented:

    – Fulfilleds: they are organized, self-confident, intellectual, mature and satisfied.

    – Believers: they are literal, law-abiding, loyal, conservative, and practical.

  - Status oriented:

    – Achievers: they are non-conventional, brand conscious, and realistic, oriented by their career/achievements.

    – Strivers: they are enthusiastic, sociable, modern, and insecure about themselves.

- Action oriented:

  – Experiencers: they are impatient, impulsive, spontaneous, young, and enthusiastic.

  – Makers: they are self-sufficient, practical and family oriented.

  2. By resources:

  – Innovators: they are independent, leaders, risk-takers, triumphant, and active.

  – Survivors: they are cautious, conservative, conformists, with low income and low education.

- Purchasing behavior (also called behavioral by some authors): dividing the market according to its purchasing behavior characteristics, such as motivation or reasoning behind the purchase of a product. For example, if we know someone is buying a product for pleasure the Marketing Mix strategy should be focused on positioning that feature.

Based on this author's marketing experience, segmentation could be done into two categories:

- *Need satisfied by the product.* If the market is divided understanding that one single product satisfies different needs, then a strategy may be designed to cater to different market segments in a more straightforward manner. For example, a postgraduate course is a product that, having exactly the same characteristics, may be offered to a market that might make the purchasing decision for very different reasons. Some customers or students might enroll to satisfy their need for security of employment because they would hold an academic degree that endorses their training. Perhaps other people decide to continue their studies to satisfy their need for recognition. Some others may do so for self-actualization purposes, believing that having a higher academic level will make them feel more satisfied with themselves. Another group may enroll for a sense of belonging because they would have a group of people to relate and socialize with for some time. Upon close observation, we realize it is the same product or service, but that it satisfies different needs with a different marketing strategy for each segment, and also with a different set of direct competitors in each segment. In the case of employment security, the competitor is in any other training course. As for self-actualization, there are many activities that bring a sense of self-actualization to people, such as marriage, having children, having their own business, writing a book, planting a tree, being altruistic, or teaching a class. Those who look for a sense of belonging find competing products in social, sports, and cultural clubs. Segmentation of a market following the needs being satisfied by the product will strengthen each of the variables of the Marketing Mix.

- *Positioning.* This concept will be described further on as the fourth step of marketing. However, within the second step, market segmentation, positioning is fitting in marketing terms, not based on the characteristics designed by the organization, or by those of the market, but for how the market actually perceives the characteristics of the product. Dividing the market according to positioning will eliminate the damage caused by a customer that doesn't belong to the segment. Can you imagine that someone who does not belong to the segment you are trying to cater to communicates their experience with your product through social networks or by word of mouth? That would be absolutely negative! On the other hand, imagine the advantages of knowing exactly how each segment of the market perceives your product. This would be very convenient for designing a strategy fitted for each of them.

Focusing on certain characteristics of the product, the market may be segmented as follows:

- Frequency of use. Dividing consumers of our product based on how often they use it.

- Usage pattern. Dividing customers according to the use they give to the product.

- Desired benefits

- Failure of attributes

- Others. Brand loyalty, purchase pattern, price sensitivity, and average of use.

Step 3. Marketing Mix

External variables

It is at the third step of Marketing where Marketing students will actually apply what they learned during most of their school years; namely, the tools used to design what the experts call the Marketing Mix—or what this author considers the Marketing Strategy, that is nothing else but the design of the four internal variables of the market: Product, Price, Place, and Promotion.

Although they taught us in school that these are the market variables that we should design, there are others that should be considered part of the Marketing Plan and are out of the company's scope of action. They are the external market variables that affect our strategy even if we have no control over them. These are:

- Macroeconomics. For example, exchange rates impact most of the products traded in our country, because only a small number of goods may be produced without the need for imported inputs.

- Government. The decisions made by the government, and the leadership style they have, may impact the industry in which a product is present. For example, government spending in certain sectors may affect other sectors negatively.

- Legal aspect. Legislation may affect our product, because any changes to the legal instruments may limit the sale of our product, the use of a certain input, or may even ban its use. In Mexico, for example, the law that bans smoking in bars and restaurants impacted the hospitality industry because the average purchase of smokers was higher than that of non-smokers.

- Competition. Competition from products that are similar or substitutes to our product is still an external variable that should be considered during the design of the marketing strategy. By analyzing the marketing mix of our competitors, for example, we could make our product different to theirs.

- Culture. The culture of a place may affect the acceptance of a product.

- Environment. The conditions of the environment may limit the access to purchase a product.

- Technology. Technological progress is forcing products to adapt to technology.

These variables are sometimes more relevant than the 4Ps, since predicting or analyzing their effect on the 4Ps may lead the company to greater profits.

A change in the macroeconomic conditions, such as an exchange rate variation of the U.S. dollar against the peso, may put the prices of domestic products out of competition or, on the contrary, may benefit their sale. A change of perspective from the government decision-makers—given their professional and political background—may have a positive or negative influence on demand, the way is happening in the current Mexican context as of the last presidential term. In this time, products related to security have had the highest demand from the government, and the investment made in them has increased as well.

A legal decision may have a drastic influence too, as evidenced by the 11 structural reforms promoted by the president in office that will definitely result in changes in consumption. With regards to the Tax Reform, it shall be noted that its purpose is to increase the number of taxpayers, thus, many products will increase their price because of an increase in tax rates. The Educational Reform will increase the demand for education institutions since teachers will need further training to be qualified to teach. As for the Telecommunications Reform, monopolized companies of this sector will lose profitability. The Energy Reform will bring about lower costs in energy, lowering, in turn, the cost of transportation within the product price fixing process.

The 4Ps of the Marketing Mix (Internal Variables)

On the other hand, we have the variables we could presumably control and design that are the internal variables of the market, which are the components of the strategy. What I am speaking about is:

Product

There are countless definitions of product within the marketing field. To avoid delving into all of these concepts, we will make a generalization by stating that the product variable is anything subject to be exchanged or sold.

For example, Kotler has what he calls a basic offering: goods, services, experiences, people, places, properties, organizations, information, and ideas.

According to Stanton, a product is a collection of recognizable attributes. For example, any product near you may be distinguished as a collection of attributes, such as color, size, texture, etc., which are recognized as a whole under a name, for example, a lamp, a pencil, a marker, a soda.

Lovelock, in his book *Services Marketing,* says that there isn't a product that is 100% tangible, nor is there a service that is 100% intangible. Every product requires complementary products and services for it to be commercialized, and every service needs products and services, as well, for it to be commercialized.

For example, a university sells the service of education, but this service could not take place if it weren't for other complementary products such as classrooms, blackboards, computers; and other added services such as counseling, library services, cafeteria, computer software, finance services, etc....

A few of the characteristics of a product, among many others that marketers should manage and design, are:

- Brand
- Color
- Size
- Packaging
- Wrapping
- Design

- Guarantee

- Development of new products

Ideally, each of these attributes is designed based on the information collected from the market. For the brand and other characteristics, a concept test is usually carried out to determine the names that are most liked by the target market.

Life Cycle of a Product

The behavior of the demand for a product goes through 4 stages that most authors call the product life cycle stages:

- Introduction. There is no direct competition because the product is new and it is characterized by a large investment in its promotion.

- Growth. A few competitors turn up, it would be the ideal stage for our product because there is a small number of competitors and the product is already positioned.

- Saturation. The market is saturated with competitors and the contribution margin is minimal.

- Decline. Demand is very low and the product is on the verge of disappearing unless it is made different or modified. There are too many competitors.

DuPont's 4 routes strategy to expand sales (Extending the product life cycle)

To extend the product's lifecycle and get demand for that product to remain the same or increase, DuPont developed and followed four routes, achieving its purpose of extending the life cycle of nylon to prevent decline.

1. Promoting a more frequent use of the product among current users: In DuPont's case, there was a promotion of the social need for women to wear stockings.

2. Developing more diverse uses of the product among current users: DuPont promoted fashion and elegance by offering tinted and patterned hosiery.

3. Creating new users for the product by increasing the market: Through the creation of hosiery lines for teenagers and children.

4. Finding new users for the basic material: Nylon was then used in rugs, tires, and pillows.

Price

The price variable in marketing has the purpose of fixing a value to anything that can be exchanged. A value that is fair for the market and at the same time makes a profit to have a relationship where the customers get what they need and the company makes a profit by selling it. When fixing a price, it is important to take into consideration two theories that are related to this variable:

Accounting Theory

This theory gives the following formula for price fixing:

- Total Income (Price x Units Sold) = Total Cost (Fixed Cost + Variable Cost) + Profit (Percentage fixed depending on the characteristics, such as the type of product)

- Follows the trend of lowering costs and increasing the profit.

All the costs incurred for the production and sale of the product are calculated in the price. It shall be noted that the costs that cause the greatest burden are the fixed costs because they are paid regardless of the product being produced or not; on the other hand, variable costs increase only when an additional unit is produced.

Now, using the formula above, how would you calculate the price of your product?

Fixing a price is not a simple task, but let us try to illustrate how to do it with the variables used in that formula. Beginning with the fixed costs: the main challenge of incorporating them into the calculation is that they can vary in timing. For example, the electricity bill is paid every two months, the rent every two weeks, the water bill every month—these are variables that cannot be added accordingly because they are each measured in a different way. However, in our example, let us pretend that the payments I make are fixed, done on a monthly basis, and are the following:

Electricity: $10,000

Water: $1,000

Rent: $5,000

Advertising: $10,000

Raw materials: $5,000

Salaries: $15,000

The sum equals a total monthly fixed cost of $46,000.

Each product sold includes a key that costs $5, and for every item sold the seller gets a $2 commission. Therefore, the variable cost of selling the item would be $7.

With those inputs, the production capacity is of 1000 units of the product.

You want to have a profit of 10%

To find the Price (P) in the Total Income (TI) formula, we get that:

$1000P = CF (\$46,000) + CV (\$7 \times 1000 \text{ units} = \$7,000) + UT (1000 \text{ units} \times 0.1 \text{ profit} \times P) =$

$1000P = 53000 - 100P$

$P = 53000/900 = \$58.88$

Economic Theory

- The price is fixed following the Laws of Supply and Demand.

- A greater offer, maintaining a constant demand, brings the price down, and vice versa, regardless of the costs inherent in the production and sale.

Under this light, the trend is to increase demand, because this would allow for the profits to increase as well, without restrictions.

The following chart shows how the Break-Even Price—where there are no earnings but no loss either—is set at the point where offer meets demand, and it also determines the number of units to produce.

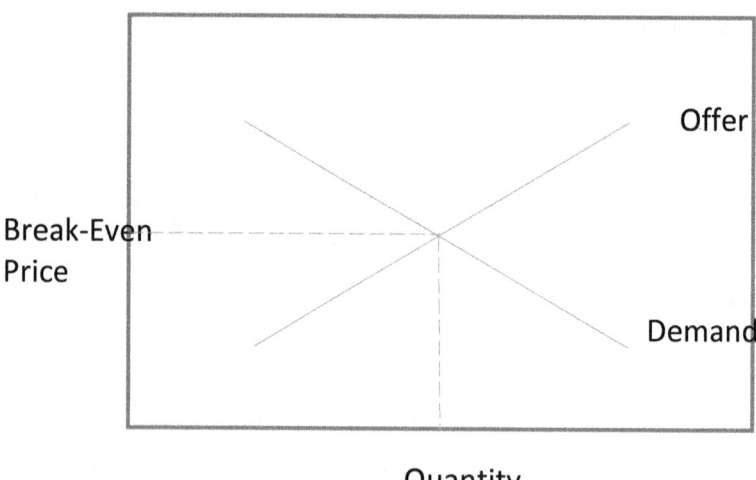

Quantity

Pricing decisions to be made:

- **Price fixing**

- **Price discrimination**

- **Credit terms**

- **Payment period**

- **Complements**

- **Discounts**

Place

Place means the location where the exchange happens, where the sale takes place. It can be a real, electronic, or virtual place. The decisions to be made for the place variable are all those that make the product available to customers, that bring it within their reach for purchase and use. Some of the characteristics marketers have to manage in the place variable are:

- **Location**

- **Coverage**

- **Stock**

- **Transportation**

- **Logistics**

- **Distribution channels**

- **Supply chains**

- **Marketing networks**

Promotion

In Lauterborn's theory, the 4Cs of marketing, promotion is called communication, which is the main purpose of this variable: communicate to the target market everything regarding the product. Among the promotion tools described by the most relevant authors are:

- Advertising: All massive and paid communication of the product.

- Personal Sales: is any direct sale made door-to-door or customer-per-customer.

- Public Relations: Are all the actions carried out by the organization to create a positive image of the brand (lobbying, donations, sponsorships, agreements, etc.). Lobbying, as I have stated in my book *Lobbying y Calbildeo: Un enfoque social para el marketing y la comunicación social*, is an activity that is performed to gain the favor of a group of people or a corporation. This highlights the fact that the Public Relations promotion tool has a broad field of action that includes all the tasks aimed at strengthening the positive image of a brand.

- Sales Promotion. All incentives that are offered to increase the sale or to introduce a product, such as discounts, coupons, loyalty plans, product partnership, etc...

- Propaganda (Stanton). Is every massive and free communication of the product, and may be either positive or negative. For example, if there is a very relevant action that leads to the brand being advertised in mass media, without having to pay for it, it is also known as propaganda. Other authors define propaganda as the spreading of ideas.

- Direct Marketing (Kotler). Any direct communication (via e-mail, telephone, SMS, etc.).

Propaganda and Direct Marketing are considered promotional tools only by Stanton and Kotler, respectively.

Step 4. Positioning

The fourth step, positioning, results when the marketing mix has been implemented for a certain market segment.

Positioning

The researcher Jack Trout coined this term and defined it as: "the place that a product or service has in the mind of consumers." The information that enters our minds does so through the five senses, which is why positioning is based on the perception the market has about our brand.

Aside from giving this mental process the name of positioning, Trout also suggests measuring it to have some mental snapshots.

"What you really want to get is a quick snapshot of the perceptions that exist in the mind, not deep thoughts. What you're after are the perceptual strengths and weaknesses of you and your competitors as they exist in the minds of the target group of customers.

Our preferred research method is listing the basic attributes in a category and asking people to grade them on a 1 to 10 scale. We do this for each competitor. The purpose is to detect which one possesses this or that idea or concept within a category.

Let us take the toothpaste category as an example: there are at least six attributes about this product: cavity prevention, flavor, whitening, breath protection, natural ingredients, cutting-edge technology. The Crest brand is based on cavity protection, Aim on its flavor, Ultrabrite on its whitening power, and Close-Up on breath protection.

Lately, Tom's of Maine has prevailed for its natural ingredients, while Mentadent has become a relevant competitor due to its technology with baking soda and peroxide. Each brand has an attribute, the trick is to determine beforehand which attribute you want to use to take over minds. And research should be a road map to get to people's minds, but avoiding the perception of your competitors."

This suggestion tends to be useful in market research to collect information on which are the segments being catered given the perception of the market, and to know what the perception of our brand is as well. We could be dealing with a product of the highest quality and the best technology, aimed at the market segment with the highest purchasing power; but if the segment does not perceive the product as such, a variable of the Marketing Mix is not in line with the perception the market has of the characteristics of the product.

It may be the case, for example, where a communication or distribution channel is not in line with the characteristics of that product, or it may be that the price gives the perception of a product of low quality.

Marketing Is Building Confidence

When a student asks me, and with very good reason, what is my definition of marketing after all the years of teaching experience I have under my belt in this field, I reply without hesitation that marketing is "building confidence."

Most become mesmerized with my statement, because at first, my definition seems lacking logic, and all of them give me a quizzical look demanding an explanation, which I elaborate by saying: "Confidence is a synonym of marketing."

Would you buy a brand of food that doesn't give you confidence? Would you go to a doctor who doesn't give you confidence? Would you drive a car that doesn't give you confidence? Would you marry someone who doesn't give you confidence? In a nutshell, to get to the exchange, you need confidence. Marketing is that collection of actions that will influence the generation or bolstering of confidence. Therefore, anything that undermines confidence contributes to damaging a brand's image and weakening its positioning.

The next question would obviously be:

What is confidence?

To know how confidence is built, we will not go into terminological detail of other areas or fields, we will simply define confidence in general, empirically and not scientifically. The Oxford Dictionary defines it as: "The feeling or belief that one can have faith in or rely on someone or something," for this reason, confidence is about keeping expectations with the certainty that one can get what one wants. Another more prominent definition of confidence is: "excessive familiarity or liberty." This excessive familiarity between our customers and us, and vice versa, is what we marketers are after. Stephen Covey, in his book *7 Habits of Highly Effective People* suggests creating win-win relationships. This is a confidence booster because customers perceive they are getting something valuable. He also promotes relationship marketing, because a company whose purpose is only one-way winning will only build distrust among the market.

This is it: the one that generates and builds confidence is the one who makes the most sales. Confidence in a good product, at a reasonable price, but overall confidence in a fair price for what is expected to be received, coming from a brand that will stand for the quality of the product at all times. And the term "fairness" does not always mean the same for the consumer as for the seller, it could be the case where the consumer does not belong to the brand's market segment.

The dictionary also defines confidence in commercial or exchange terms, as follows: a pact or agreement made in private and in confidence between two or more people, particularly between traders or merchants, the pact is of buying what is being demanded and getting the benefits of it.

In conclusion, confidence, whether seen as a feeling (sensation) or a state of mind, is built on the foundation of the information that enters our brain.

How does all the data that becomes information and creates a product image enter our brain?

Through our senses, obviously. That is why the building of confidence is based on the information that enters our minds through our senses, which are directly linked to perception, understanding it as an inner feeling that results from a material impression that takes place in our senses.

Perception follows the brain stimuli caused by the five senses—sight, smell, touch, hearing, and taste—that make up a physical reality of the environment. Marketing should work on this concept, because the difference between having confidence in a brand or not occurs in the way in which information becomes known through the senses.

Imagine you wish to know how the weather is in a city where a member of your family lives. You give them a call and ask, but at that moment this family member is in his office with the air conditioning set so low that he is shivering with cold, he will surely say that the weather is just fine, even when outside the temperature is over 100°F.

The same goes for marketing. That is why one of its myths is that it tricks people into something because it is very likely that there are unethical people who communicate sensorial benefits that your product cannot deliver. But this cannot build confidence or long-term relationships, which is the ultimate purpose of marketing. Abraham Lincoln said: "You cannot fool all the people all of the time."

The only purpose that you have, as a reader of this book, is to ethically communicate all the qualities of your product, because you have put hard work into creating a high-quality product. But do not rule out that some information that is coming through the senses might be creating a wrong perception about the quality of your product, just like in the air conditioning example.

That is why the job of a marketer is to create among the customers the image that we want through perception, which is known as positioning. Kotler shows us the difference between needs, wants, and demand, to find the scope of action of marketing, and clear up the myth that it creates needs.

According to Kotler, the work of marketing is to shape these wants—which involves direct action on the perception or actions at a mind level—in such a way that if a person has a need for self-actualization, marketing must act in the minds of potential consumers—or of those who represent the demand—to make them choose my brand to satisfy their need, over some other substitute product that may not have the same characteristics or fall in the same business sector as my product.

The above is in line with the assumption made in this book that marketers should build confidence based on positioning because perception allows information to enter our minds, where wants can be shaped. It is in our minds where the feeling of confidence is created. Maybe that is why this old myth of marketing being equal to advertising is deeply rooted, because it is the visible aspect of the marketing strategy, the one in contact with the senses remotely, without knowing the product.

However, if we make an analysis, that advertising is always in line with the objectives of marketing, at least in brands that are backed up by a well-rounded marketing strategy, and unlike those cases where brands are transmitting messages without a defined goal. That is why Jack Trout, who coined the positioning concept, suggests in his book that we carry out a market research on the perceived attributes to have a real idea of the placement of the product or brand in the minds of our market segment.

Perhaps the strategy is designed for the positioning of a luxury item, but what people are perceiving is a cheap item. Maybe you are investing in a high-quality item, but your advertising strategy is being transmitted through a media with a low rating and that might be generating a contradictory perception, o maybe a message is quite vulgar or not creative enough and is causing that effect. That is why positioning feeds on all the marketing variables.

In short, confidence will boost customers' Lifetime Value, a concept developed by Arthur Middleton Hughes. Lifetime Value is how a lifetime customer yields greater income or benefits for a company than one-time customers, which is why incentives—not only economical but attention and focus as well—should be aimed at the group with the highest retention.

Every marketing action has the purpose of contributing to building the confidence between seller and consumer, even those actions that we believe don't have a tangible or short-term impact. For example, allocating a percentage of the proceeds from the sale of our product to a charitable cause will not be translated into greater profits in the short term. On the contrary, income will be reduced. However, this public relations action will build confidence among the brand's customers, generating lifetime customers that trust the brand.

These concepts are the product of the author's teaching experience and it was God's motivation that made him put them together in this book.

Bibliography

- Aaker, David. *Investigación de mercados.* McGraw Hill.

- Covey, Stephen. *Los 7 hábitos de la gente eficaz.* Covey Leadership Center, Paidós Plural, 2003.

- *Definition of 'Confidence'.* Oxford Dictionaries. 2016. Oxford University Press. 3 February 2016. <http://www.oxforddictionaries.com/us/definition/american _english/confidence>

- De Parres Cárdenas, Verania, trans. *Marketing Research: An Applied Orientation.* By Malhotra, Naresh K. México: Prentice Hall Hispanoamericana, Georgia Institute of Technology, 1997.

- Gonzalez, Ignacio, et al. *Lobbying y cabildeo.* México: Gasca, 2008.

- Hughes, Arthur M. *Strategic Database Marketing.* New York: McGraw-Hill, 1994.

- Kotler, Philip. *Dirección de Marketing.* México: Pearson Educación, 2001.

- Levitt, Theodore. "Exploit the Product Life Cycle" in *Harvard Business Review,* 1965.

- Lovelock, Christopher. *Mercadotecnia de Servicios.* Prentice Hall, 1997.

- Ramírez, Edmundo. "La segmentación por estilo de vida". México: AMAI, 1997.

- Ries, Al. *Focus: The Future of Your Company Depends on It.* September 27, 2005

- Stanton, William. *Fundamentos de Mercadotecnia.* México: McGraw Hill, 1998.

- Trout, Jack. *El Nuevo Posicionamiento.* McGraw-Hill, 1996.

www.ingramcontent.com/pod-product-compliance
Lightning Source LLC
Chambersburg PA
CBHW070423190526
45169CB00003B/1384